DATE DUE   SEP 0 5

GAYLORD			PRINTED IN U.S.A.

Fred Read
the
Red Book

Pam Scheunemann

JACKSON COUNTY LIBRARY SERVICES
MEDFORD, OREGON 97501

Published by SandCastle™, an imprint of ABDO Publishing Company, 4940 Viking Drive, Edina, Minnesota 55435.

Printed in the United States.

Photo credits: Corbis Images, Digital Vision, Eyewire Images, PhotoDisc

Library of Congress Cataloging-in-Publication Data

Scheunemann, Pam, 1955–
    Fred read the red book / Pam Scheunemann.
       p. cm. -- (Homophones)
    Includes index.
    Summary: Photographs and simple text introduce homophones, words that sound alike but are spelled differently and have different meanings.
    ISBN 1-57765-745-4
     1. English language--Homonyms--Juvenile literature. [1. English language--Homonyms.] I. Title. II. Series.

PE1595 .S35 2002
428.1--dc21

2001053316

The SandCastle concept, content, and reading method have been reviewed and approved by a national advisory board including literacy specialists, librarians, elementary school teachers, early childhood education professionals, and parents.

Let Us Know

After reading the book, SandCastle would like you to tell us your stories about reading. What is your favorite page? Was there something hard that you needed help with? Share the ups and downs of learning to read. We want to hear from you! To get posted on the ABDO Publishing Company Web site, send us email at:

sandcastle@abdopub.com

About SandCastle™
Nonfiction books for the beginning reader

- Basic concepts of phonics are incorporated with integrated language methods of reading instruction. Most words are short, and phrases, letter sounds, and word sounds are repeated.

- Book levels are based on the ATOS™ for Books formula. Other considerations for readability include the number of words in each sentence, the number of characters in each word, and word lists based on curriculum frameworks.

- Full-color photography reinforces word meanings and concepts.

- "Words I Can Read" list at the end of each book teaches basic elements of grammar, helps the reader recognize the words in the text, and builds vocabulary.

- Reading levels are indicated by the number of flags on the castle.

SandCastle uses the following definitions for this series:

- Homographs: words that are spelled the same but sound different and have different meanings. *Easy memory tip: "-graph"= same look*

- Homonyms: words that are spelled and sound the same but have different meanings. *Easy memory tip: "-nym"= same name*

- Homophones: words that sound alike but are spelled differently and have different meanings. *Easy memory tip: "-phone"= sound alike*

Look for more SandCastle books in these three reading levels:

Level 1 (one flag)	**Level 2** (two flags)	**Level 3** (three flags)

Grades Pre-K to K 5 or fewer words per page	**Grades K to 1** 5 to 10 words per page	**Grades 1 to 2** 10 to 15 words per page

Note: Some pages in this book contain more than five words in order to more clearly convey the concept of the book.

rose   rows

Homophones are words that sound alike but are spelled differently and have different meanings.

Joe **reads** with his mom.

Reeds grow near water.

Amy knows the **right** answer.

Mary likes to **write**.

Cindy **rode** with the puppies.

A **road** is for travel.

Ali played a **role**.

Mark likes to **roll**.

Emma likes to **raise** flowers.

The sun has **rays**.

This tree has a big root.

This family picks their route.

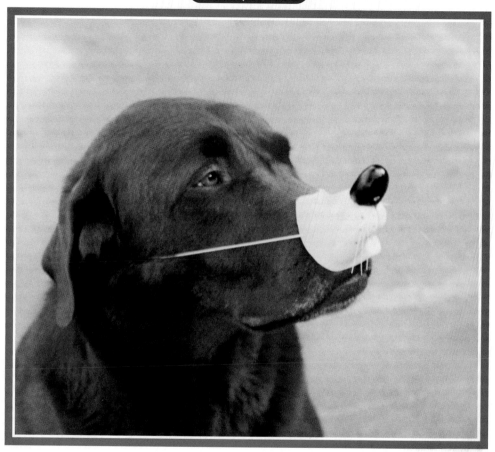

This nose is not **real**.

We **reel** in our fish.

It **rains** on my face.

What does Lisa hold?

(the reins)

Words I Can Read

Nouns

A noun is a person, place, or thing

answer (AN-sur) p. 8

face (FAYSS) p. 20

family (FAM-uh-lee)
  p. 17

fish (FISH) p. 19

flowers (FLOU-urz)
  p. 14

homophones
  (HOME-uh-fonez)
  p. 5

meanings
  (MEE-ningz) p. 5

mom (MOM) p. 6

nose (NOHZ) p. 18

puppies (PUHP-eez)
  p. 10

rays (RAYZ) p. 15

reeds (REEDZ) p. 7

reins (RAYNZ) p. 21

road (ROHD) p. 11

role (ROHL) p. 12

root (ROOT) p. 16

rose (ROHZ) p. 4

route (ROOT) p. 17

rows (ROHZ) p. 4

sun (SUHN) p. 15

travel (TRAV-uhl) p. 11

tree (TREE) p. 16

water (WAW-tur) p. 7

words (WURDZ) p. 5

Proper Nouns

A proper noun is the name
of a person, place, or thing

Ali (AL-ee) p. 12

Amy (AY-mee) p. 8

Cindy (SIN-dee) p. 10

Emma (EM-uh) p. 14

Joe (JOH) p. 6

Lisa (LEE-suh) p. 21

Mark (MARK) p. 13

Mary (MAIR-ee) p. 9

Verbs

A verb is an action or being word

are (AR) p. 5

does (DUHZ) p. 21

grow (GROH) p. 7

has (HAZ) pp. 15, 16

have (HAV) p. 5

hold (HOHLD) p. 21

is (IZ) pp. 11, 18

knows (NOHZ) p. 8

likes (LIKESS)
　　pp. 9, 13, 14

picks (PIKSS) p. 17

played (PLAYD) p. 12

rains (RAYNZ) p. 20

raise (RAYZ) p. 14

reads (REEDZ) p. 6

reel (REEL) p. 19

rode (ROHD) p. 10

roll (ROHL) p. 13

sound (SOUND) p. 5

spelled (SPELD) p. 5

write (RITE) p. 9

23

Picture Words

rains

reins

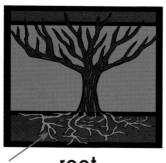

root

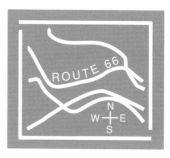

route